The Final

Beyond A Reasonable Doubt
By John J. Briggle, ©2020

The Final Answer Is… THE BIBLE IS TRUE!

Beyond A Reasonable Doubt

By John J. Briggle

©2020

The Final Answer Is... THE BIBLE IS TRUE!
Table of Contents

DEDICATION

When an author keeps writing books as I have been doing lately, it is difficult to add new names in the list of those a book should be dedicated to. Like, when an Academy Award winner takes the stage to thank all those who put him/her onstage to accept the coveted Oscar statue, my list can go on and on of those who made this "Oscar" possible.

Of course, I must begin with my wife Ginny, then my children Benjamin, Christopher, and Kristen, then my grandchildren, my seven brothers and sisters, and then the hook comes from the side of the stage to cut off my winded but necessary gratitude.

Oh, but before I leave the stage, I would also like to dedicate this book to my loving parents, Joan and Albert, both deceased, for whom none of this would be possible.

Wait, there is more: to my spiritual leaders Reverend Harold Raines of Monroe Full Gospel Church, Pastor Lillian Easterly-Smith and her husband Mike, and to Phil Norcom of Last Days Institute, Chaplain Richard Baldwin and to Elder Ralphonzo Martin, and many others. The Lord God has taken me through a journey for which many other pastors, ministers of His Word, deacons, and other honorary ones have crossed my path, and I have learned so much, so quickly, and so deeply.

Thanks to every one of you and may the God of all grace, mercy, peace, and love bless you abundantly. May all of us receive the call to the biggest stage, in His presence and all His glory. Amen.

"Therefore, having been justified by faith, we have peace with God through our Lord Jesus Christ, through whom also we have access by faith into this grace in which we stand, and rejoice in hope of the glory of God. And not only that, but we also glory in tribulations, knowing that tribulation produces perseverance, and perseverance, character; and character, hope. Now hope does not disappoint, because the love of God has been poured out in our hearts by the Holy Spirit who was given to us." **Rom 5:1-5**

INTRODUCTION

The Holy Bible is true because it says it is. *"All Scripture is given by inspiration of God...."* **2 Tim 3:16** Is that enough proof that is sufficient to believe in an autonomous GOD of the universe who created all there is and beyond? If one believes in the Bible, maybe the answer is a resounding yes, but what gets one to that point? That is the theme of this book, to solidify and defend what you already know to be the truth.

There are already many excellent Christian apologetic books available and I hope this one is unique in its own way. One can never be prepared enough in this world because new questions are being thrown at us daily, many with newly discovered, so-called evidences that challenge even the strongest believers to hold fast to their faith.

The evidences included herein to defend the Holy Bible as the inerrant Word of God are indisputable, yet resisted as truth by those who simply do not want to believe because they don't want to change their guilt-filled ways, their self-indulgent behavior, or their prideful self-gratifying, self-existence. Others may not want to believe what is so obvious because of indoctrination by some other belief system. There is always time to change as long as you have a breath, the very breath that our living God has given you.

After reading this book, when someone asks you, "Why are you are Christian; why do you believe the Bible to be true?", you will *"always be ready to give a defense to anyone who asks you the reason for the hope that is in you...."*

God bless you all.

"Oh, give thanks to the LORD, for He is good! For His mercy endures forever. Oh, give thanks to the God of gods! For His mercy endures forever. Oh, give thanks to the Lord of lords! For His mercy endures forever: To Him who alone does great wonders, For His mercy endures forever;" **Psa 136:1-4**

Chapter 1: THE TRUTH SERUM

"Sanctify them with Your Word, Your Word is truth" **Jn 17:17**

This chapter is, in part, from my previous book *CREATION 101: A Study Guide To The Creation of the Earth, Universe, and Beyond.* It is important to establish what truth is, a basis for any further discussion in seeking absolute truth and the Holy Bible.

Today's worldview is that there is no such thing as absolute truth. We each have a right to an opinion, and if we believe that opinion is true, then, there you go, it's true! What's true for you is not true for me and vice-versa. Philosophers refer to this as relativism and many are okay with it as truth becomes a self-infused reality, many times formed by social and cultural processes. Too often truth is based on intellectual concepts and incomplete facts.

A fact *should* be a truth; a true fact is redundant. Someone may take a fact and interpret it in a way that causes possibilities of contradictions. Someone can say "2+2=5," and your questioning that assessment is your limited reasoning that we may eventually discover that *is* true. A fact should be a verifiable truth, but that is where this whole convoluted discussion gets twisted as two people can dissect a fact and come up with two different conclusions. For instance, someone can look at a fossil and conclude it is over two billion years old, whereas another person can explain it as a rapid compression and less than ten thousand years old. The same fossil *fact*, two different conclusions and those conclusions become *fact* in that person's mind as to how the fossil came to be.

Can two opposites both be true? The *fact* is no. Someone may try to justify 2+2=5 in his/her mind, but 2+2=4 is an absolute, verifiable truth; both cannot be true. This is not an opinion but a carved-in-granite fact.

Also, emotion and compassion do not make an idea any truer than oleo margarine being the same as butter. Many people get all charged up about something and the tone of their voice can make it seem like it must be true; their passion makes it truth.

Colleges and universities are teaching our young minds some incredibly stupid things these days. Laurie Rubel, a mathematics education ***professor*** at New York's Brooklyn College, tweeted the following: "The idea that math (or data) is culturally neutral or in any way objective is a MYTH." Rubel added, "along with the 'of course math is neutral because 2+2=4 trope are the related (and creepy) 'math is pure' and 'protect math.' This kind of statement that 2+2=4 "reeks of white supremacist patriarchy." [cont.] "I'd [sic] rather think on nurturing people & protecting the planet (with math in service of them goals)," the professor added.[1]

Absurdity, but that is where the world is headed and college professors are leading the way, so far away from any absolute truth.

My geometry teacher in high school filled an entire chalkboard with formulas and calculations with a conclusion that 2=1. All of us student "geniuses" marveled that our teacher was able to prove an absolute and academic principle that 2=2 could be wrong. Obviously, we were supposed to have enough aspirin and duct tape to keep our heads from exploding and find the flaw in all the chalk scribblings.

The Law of Non-Contradiction: two opposites cannot both be true. Everyone has a right to his/her own opinion even though that opinion may not contain any substance of truth; opinion is not the same as truth.

If I believe that God exists and you don't, one of us is wrong. If I believe that the Holy Bible is the authentic inspired Word of God but you do not, one of us is wrong. If I believe in a Biblical heaven and hell but you don't, one of us is wrong. In any situation including those just listed, a conclusion that "What's true for you is not true for me" does not exist; it *cannot* exist.

---

[1] https://pjmedia.com/culture/tyler-o-neil/2020/08/13/math-professor-the-224-trope-reeks-of-white-supremacist-patriarchy-n789098, Aug 23, 2020

You likely have heard, "Christianity may be true for you but not for me." Can that statement be true? Answer: No. If Christianity is true, it is true for everyone. No opinion is expressed or implied in that statement.

You may or may not be a Christian reading this book, but a must read for every person, besides the Holy Bible, (and my other books) is the book: "I Don't Have Enough Faith To Be An Atheist,"[2] by Norma L. Geisler and Frank Turek. It is one of the most powerful Christian apologetics books one can read. Frank Turek participates in many debates globally with the most influential atheists and his style and acumen are incredible (see your favorite search engine).

Some may say each has a right to his/her own spirituality and that is *their* truth. Everyone *does* have a right to their own opinion and spirituality, but it does not make it truth. Each one of us has the free will choice to worship in Christianity, Islam, Hinduism, Buddhism, Satanism, or the like. Only ONE is correct. If the God of the Bible is as the Holy Bible says He is, belief in any other will *not* get him/her through the pearly gates of heaven no matter how strong their belief in those other said religions.

"There is salvation in no other (Jesus), *for there is no other name under heaven given among men by which we must be saved."* **Acts 12:4**

If someone does not believe the earth is round, that insistence doesn't change the reality of the truth that the earth is round. If God is the Intelligent Designer of all creation but you don't believe in such a God, that cannot negate the truth that He is outside of time, before all things, who was and is and is to come and *is* the Creator of all things. Just because someone does not believe in something does not cancel its existence. All this is elementary, but many people believe their opinion is all that matters, have no problem sharing it, and their opinion is powerful enough to be an excuse not to believe in any absolute truth and

---

[2] Norman L. Geisler, Frank Turek, *I Don't Have Enough Faith To Be An Atheist*, Crossway Publications, Wheaton, IL, ©2004

changes the truth to accommodate their beliefs. Absolute truth cannot be changed to accommodate someone's opinion or belief.

God is creator over all, whether people accept or deny His existence. *"The fool has said in his heart, there is no God."* **Psa 14:1**

Consensus does not make something true, though it may be true. At one time, most believed the earth was flat, a consensus among almost everyone. We now know that not to be true. Believe it or not, there are some who still believe the earth is flat.

In "I Don't Have Enough Faith To Be An Atheist," Frank Turek assesses these truths about truth:

- ❖ Truth is discovered, not invented. It exists independent of anyone's knowledge of it. (Gravity existed before Newton's discovery of it.)
- ❖ Truth is transcultural; if something is true, it is true for all people, in all places, at all times (2+2=4 for everyone, everywhere, at every time).
- ❖ Truth is unchanging even though our *beliefs* about truth change. (When we began to believe the earth was round instead of flat, the *truth* about the earth did not change, only our *belief* about the earth changed.)
- ❖ Beliefs cannot change a fact, no matter how sincerely they are held. (Someone can sincerely believe the earth is flat, but that only makes that person sincerely mistaken.)
- ❖ Truth is not affected by the attitude of the one professing it. (An arrogant person does not make the truth he professes false. A humble person does not make the error he professes true.)
- ❖ All truths are absolute truths. Even truths that seem to be relative are really absolute. (For example, "I, Frank Turek, feel warm on November 20, 2003" may appear to be a

relative truth, but it is actually absolutely true for everyone, that Frank Turek had the sensation of warmth on that day.) In short, contrary *beliefs* are possible, but contrary *truths* are not possible. We can *believe* everything is true, but we cannot *make* everything true.[3]

Another law of logic is the Law of Excluded Middle wherein something either *is* or *is not*. Very similar to the Law of Non-Contradiction, something cannot *be* if it *is not*. God either *is*, or He *is not*. God either created the world and everything that exists, or He did not. There is no middle ground where we can camp and know we are resting in a truth.

Truth has dangerously become whatever anyone wants to believe and that has the potential to divide families, nations, and the Body of Christ, His Church of believers. Even when it comes to the Holy Bible, people want to drift away to accommodate their own reasoning or theories that contradict the Word of God. Many well-meaning Christians treat the Holy Bible like a smorgasbord, picking and choosing only what they want, ignoring the Word that convicts them.

Scientists are human and, believe it or not, are very often wrong. Any "new" revelations regarding anything in the Bible is a different perspective or perception by man. That is one reason this book is so important, a reminder that God's Word cannot be changed or added to.

> *"For I testify to everyone who hears the words of the prophecy of this book* [the Holy Bible]*: If anyone adds to these things, God will add to him the plagues that are written in this book; and if anyone takes away from the words of this book of this prophecy, God shall take away his part from the Book of Life, from the holy city, and from the things which are written in this book."* **Rev 22:18,19**

---

[3] Ibid, Pg 37,38

"Do not add to His words, lest He rebuke you, and you be found a liar." **Prov 30:6**

I have heard it argued that warnings like the above only apply to the book of Revelation, or the writings in Proverbs, but *"**All Scripture** is given by inspiration of God, and is profitable for doctrine, for reproof, for correction, for instruction in righteousness, that the man of God may be perfect and complete, lacking nothing."* **2 Tim 3:16** If it is worthy to be in the Holy Bible, it is God-breathed, the *inspired* Word of God.

Simple Indisputable Fact: Law of Non-Contradiction Applied

If you are an atheist, agnostic, or otherwise deny that there is an Intelligent Designer, or God, and you are correct, then none of this matters; you and I and everyone else are in the same boat and when we die and are buried or cremated—poof! Gone, no eternal consequences.

But, if there *is* an Intelligent Designer we know as God of the universe and beyond, and if the Holy Bible is the truly inspired Word of this Sovereign God and His way is the only way into heaven, we are *not* all in the same boat when we die. Some will go to heaven and be with Him in all His glory forever, and those who deny Jesus as our Lord and Savior will spend eternity in the torments of hell.

Both options cannot be true. There is no, "That's your opinion," or "Maybe, but…." I pray you come to His throne of grace and accept Him before it's too late. There is still time.

If the Holy Bible is true, these two Bible verses are paramount: *"I am the Way, the Truth, and the Life. No one comes to the Father but by Me (Jesus)."* **Jn 14:6** *"There is salvation in no other, for there is no other name under heaven (Jesus) given among men by which we must be saved."* **Acts 12:4**

Chapter 2: IF I BELIEVE THE BIBLE, SO SHOULD YOU

One of the greatest of many wonderful gifts God has given us is the gift of free will, a choice to do whatever we want. Some of those choices are bad; some of those are blatantly in defiance of God, even denying Him and His existence. No one can force you to make a choice you don't want to make, especially one that Jesus spoke: *"If anyone desires to come after Me, let him deny himself, and take up his cross, and follow Me. For whoever desires to save his life will lose it, but whoever loses his life for My sake will find it. Deny yourself, take up your cross, and follow Me."* **Matt 16:24** That's an order of self-denial not everyone is willing to commit to. If there is no God, it does not matter anyway.

But if there is a God? Is Jesus God manifested in the flesh, the only begotten Son of God, He who takes away the sins of the world, who was crucified, buried in a grave, and arose after three days in a carefully guarded tomb, and gifted us His Holy Spirit that can reside in each of us so that we can have the mind of Christ our Savior? That is a mouthful. I can tell you I believe that, but I cannot expect you to believe that based solely on me telling you to believe because I do.

I *may* get you to believe because I do, by your witnessing a change in my lifestyle, my energized new life in Christ, and the peace and joy, and my fearless desire to *"die in Christ"* that is so evident. Your belief may be based on a desire like "I want what you have" and that is available just by simply accepting Him as your Lord and Savior.

But what if I falter or revert back to my previous lifestyle of sin, depravity, and self-serving habits? Or even come to a different conclusion after serving Him as many do. "I tried that Jesus-stuff; it didn't work for me." Your faith, *my* faith, must be built on something more substantive than just a whim or possibility that God could be real, the Self-Existent One outside of time and space, who had no beginning and will always be.

My faith is built on a solid Rock and overwhelming evidence of the existence of an Intelligent Designer. No one can expect their faith to be irreversible unless there is solid evidence beyond a reasonable doubt.

That is the test in our court system, beyond a reasonable doubt. All the evidence presented, then, the jury foreman declares, "We believe…."

The expectation that just because I believe in God does not surpass the burden of proof for most people to believe. I believe so you should believe; there must be something more. There is.

If evolution is the way we are here then none of this matters, we're no different from that biting mosquito you smack through the epidermis of your flesh on your arm. Poof—gone! If there is no God of the universe, any spiritual connection we claim to have doesn't matter, our life is meaningless, except for a legacy we leave behind, perhaps making this planet a better place, but who is the judge if it is better or worse by one's short existence here on earth? Your very existence in the physical realm is destroying the planet according to some, your expelling of carbon dioxide and methane gas is damaging to the planet. Too many people creating too much pollution by their very presence.

Without God, there is no purpose in life. But wait, "I invented this perpetual-motion engine, I discovered that vaccine, I wrote that movie script, I performed in concert for over two million people worldwide, I preached the Gospel to twenty million lost souls worldwide and led thousands to the Lord…." You can see how we decide our own worth, or society does. Your absolute worth is through Jesus' eyes.

Without God there are no consequences to a heinous lifestyle of crime, hatred and racism, murder and rape, except judgment and punishment by man. Some societies think much of that is okay. Who are we to judge Hitler, Stalin, Mao, or those that followed those murderous leaders? They were only doing what their society accepted as okay.

But if there is a God of righteousness and judgment who can cast many into eternal punishment in a place called hell? If there is a loving, living God of the universe who knew us before we were born, who wants a personal relationship with us in His presence for eternity in heaven? If the Holy Bible is real with specific guidelines that we must follow to escape hell and enter heaven?

The choice of heaven or hell is not a reason to believe in Him or the Bible, but it is certainly a secondary incentive. *"I am the Way, the Truth, and the Life. No one comes to the Father except by Him."* **Jn 14:6** Your belief should be because He loves you and desires you to love Him. That being said, we are human beings and it is natural that we desire proof. Scripture verses are nice and eventually will be the *only* proof needed, but skeptics are ready to tear your faith apart at the seams.

> *"Faith is the substance of things hoped for, the evidence of things not seen."* **Heb 11:1**

What does that verse mean to you? That single verse is very deep in meaning and requires meditation. Is that verse powerful enough for you to convince others that the Bible is the authentic Word of God, though you only hope for what is not seen, and that they should believe because you do? This book will bridge that gap. You will believe with confidence and your faith will be further enriched. Then we will confidently *"Walk by faith, not by sight."* **2 Cor 5:7**

Those who do not believe in God have their own layers of blind faith, often in unchallenged hypotheses by scientists or philosophers. A couple quick questions: Where are you in your faith? Do you think you are practicing blind faith? After reading this book, you will realize there is no need to feel meek in your faith walk as evidence will convince you that one's faith in Jesus, in the Holy Bible, need not be blind faith at all. The affirmation is quite overwhelming beyond a reasonable doubt.

"And now, O Lord GOD, You are God, and Your words are true, and You have promised this goodness to Your servant." **2 Sam 7:28**

Ponder this for a moment.... Why are you convinced, if you are, that the Holy Bible is the inspired Word of God, as recorded by chosen men of God to convey it to us throughout all the ages? Can you defend your belief and compassion? *"Always be ready to give an answer to everyone who asks you a reason for the hope that is in you."* **1 Pet 3:15**

Chapter 3: MY CHANGED LIFE IS PROOF OF GOD

When I became a born again Christian in 2008, I had no clue what that meant nor did I have any idea that God would use me in incredible ways beyond my own selfish ambitions. The thought had not even crossed my mind that I had signed up to "deny myself, take up my cross, and follow Him." But it happened.

This is book number seven that I have written and had published in the last four years, something I had no desire to do, not even the first one—but now, been there, done that! I had performed in a rock and roll band for many years but never considered myself a songwriter. In the short time since my deliverance, the Lord has inspired me to write over fifteen Christian songs with the flow of God's Word within each, and several secular songs. Also, a screenplay!

At my old age (67, LOL!), I was a latecomer to what God had planned for this not-so-eager servant. His plan never wavered from the beginning; I no doubt resisted. Now I am willing participant as a pastor and evangelist and a good and faithful servant of our Lord Jesus Christ, praying and listening every day to receive my next mission. My family and friends do not recognize me as the changed man I am now because of His intervention and all His blessings. I am a restored man with new life. Amen.

> *"I have been crucified with Christ; it is no longer I who live, but Christ lives in me; and the life which I now live in the flesh I live by faith in the Son of God, who loved me and gave Himself for me."* **Gal 2:20**

Many millions of people have overcome addictions in the name of Jesus. Many have been healed in the name of Jesus. Many miracles have been accomplished in the name of Jesus. Many have found peace and joy and true love in the name of Jesus. Many, many, many. I see evidence of a living, loving God every day I minister to people, lives truly changed like mine. To the many whose lives have been transformed by a simple commitment to Jesus, there is no doubt God is real, the Holy Bible is His sanctified Word, and the power of the Holy Ghost resides within each individual. Those who do not believe can't understand our commitment.

We become His testimony and witness to His Almighty power.

Is that enough evidence beyond a reasonable doubt that the Holy Bible is real and God of the Bible is the Intelligent Designer of all of this?

Nay-sayers will claim there is no such thing as a miracle, nor a supernatural change within anybody. Any equivocal change can be accomplished through secular psychological counselling, self-help books, yoga and meditation, new age transcendentalism, or other similar programs. Motivational speakers go on tours, write books, and speak how their lives were changed by a few simple steps of self-discipline that they encourage you can do, also. They proclaim success of overcoming drug or alcohol addiction can occur with various programs or professional intervention, without God in one's life, and certainly without a crazy book written by over forty ancient men over two thousand years ago. And of course, any of those personal testimonies of Jesus' intervention cannot prove anything, especially God's existence and The Holy Bible.

Okay, I get it. People desire incontestable truths, conclusive natural world explanations to overcome any gobble-de-gook supernaturalism. They want attestation by all our five senses. They want to touch and see the documentation and confirmation of proof.

I am alive today because of the love of Jesus, His intervention in my life is all I needed to extend my ability to breath the air and receive necessary sustenance He provides. Thank you, Jesus.

> *"And they overcame by the blood of the Lamb and by **the word of their testimony.**"* **Rev 19:11** Our testimony.

A previous book of mine, *CREATION 101: A Study Guide to the Creation of the Earth, Universe, and Beyond*, is a Biblical viewpoint of how everything was created and provides ample evidence that an Almighty Intelligent Designer, our God of the Holy Bible, created all of this. It is a basic apologetics book to take you to the next level of defense of the Holy Bible.

This book *The Final Answer Is...THE BIBLE IS TRUE!* is focused on the Bible, how we can be assured of its standard truths for all life, that it is the infallible Word of God. That evidence is forthcoming—read on!

Chapter 4: THE PROBABILTY IS OVERWHELMING

How do we know the Bible is true? One powerful substantiation is the number of Old Testament prophecies that have come true, verification written in the New Testament, or witnessed post-Bible Canon. The cool aspect of this proof is that we do not have to go outside Scriptures to verify its authenticity as Divinely inspired.

Certain things blow our minds when studying the accuracy of fulfilled Bible prophecy beyond the mathematics of probability. The writings of Ezekiel:

> *"In the twenty-fifth year of our captivity, at the beginning of the year, on the tenth day of the month, in the fourteenth year after the city was captured, on the very same day the hand of the LORD was upon me; and He took me there. In the visions of God, He took me into the land of Israel and set me on a very high mountain; on it toward the south was like the structure of a city."* **Eze 40:1,2**

The Bible's prophetic accuracy is incredible, even predicting that Israel would become a unified country again after so many years of being scattered around the globe, to come home to their own nation. This is one of the little-talked about fulfilled prophecies, but to the day, Israel became a nation on May 15, 1948.

"What does that mean, brother John?" The number 1260 from Revelation 11:3 is a number that repeats a pattern throughout history, particularly prophetically for the Jewish and Christian world. Many believe the 1260 assigned as *years* is all about Catholicism and the Pope's reign, but I am not going to go there. Instead, a more definitive fulfillment was, from using two patterns of 1260 years beginning when Ezekiel records:

> *"Thus says the Lord GOD: "On the day that I cleanse you from all your iniquities, I will also enable you to dwell in the cities, and the ruins shall be rebuilt. The desolate land shall be tilled instead of lying desolate in the sight of all who pass by. So they will say, '**This land that was desolate has become like the garden of Eden; and the wasted, desolate, and ruined cities are now fortified and inhabited.**'"*

This is an amazing, fulfilled prophecy including God's blessing upon the land of this once desolate, uninhabitable land which is now fertile and lush with beautiful vegetation, farming, and other valuable self-sustaining resources.

When Ezekiel measured the visionary temple recorded in Ezekiel 40 (573 B.C., with variances from their 30-day months and "catch-up" years) to Israel's reestablishment as an independent nation in 1948 is exactly two sets of 1260 years, 2520 years!

"But brother John, anyone can pull numbers out of the Bible and make it fit any prophetic claim." Yes, I agree, and many have done so to create false doctrine. God is a sharp-shooter and His omniscience is evident every time it is written *"Thus saith the LORD...."*

Let us now talk about accuracy beyond a reasonable doubt in prophecies regarding the coming Messiah. The number of fulfilled prophecies specific to Jesus vary by scholars from 200-400. The fact that one prophecy is exactly fulfilled is amazing but is not enough evidence that the Holy Bible is the inspired Word of God. But 200-400 certainly defies all objections. Barton Payne in his "Encyclopedia of Bible Prophecy" writes there are 191 prophetic messages specific to Jesus.[4]

In 1953, Peter W. Stoner, an agnostic mathematics and astronomy professor at Pasadena City College, California, gave his students a project on the study of probability. One of the students spoke up and asked about the probability of Messianic prophecies being fulfilled. Being a lukewarm believer, he thought what a great exercise to prove to students that the numbers could not substantiate without a reasonable doubt the existence of Jesus as Messiah.

In 1957, he published the results of that classroom project in his book "Science Speaks," and the probability odds exceed all measures of statistical standards. Numbers can be confusing so I will try to keep it simple. It is understood that any probability formula that is greater than a 1×10^{10} is accepted as unquestionable odds of accuracy. For his students, he picked only eight of the Messianic prophecies and the result was

---

[4] Barton Payne, Encyclopedia of Bible Prophecy, Wipf and Stock Publishers, Eugene, Oregon. 1973

declared "that any man might have lived down to the present time and fulfilled all eight prophecies is 1 in 10^{17}."[5] In real number connotation, that is 1 in 10,000,000,000,000,000,000. Crazy, huh?

The eight Scriptures used were:

(1) Messiah to be born in Bethlehem. Micah 5:2
(2) Messiah betrayed for thirty pieces of silver. Zechariah 11:12-13
(3) Messiah's clothes would be gambled away. Psalms 22:18
(4) Messiah's hands and feet would be pierced. Psalms 22:16
(5) Messiah's bones would not be broken. Psalms 34:20
(6) Messiah would be born in the tribe of Judah. Isaiah 37:31
(7) Messiah would be called from Egypt. Hosea 11:1
(8) Messiah would be buried in a rich man's grave. Isaiah 53:9

The odds of all eight coming true are virtually incomprehensible!

A common example often used to explain these incredible odds of probability is this: Suppose we filled the entire State of Texas with 100 trillion silver dollars. That would make the entire state about two feet deep in coins. Then we mark only one coin. Next, we stir-up the state full of coins so they are thoroughly mixed and random. The marked coin could be anywhere in the state in the two-foot-deep coins. Finally, we blindfold a man and let him travel the entire state to find that one random coin.

What would be the odds of him finding the marked coin in one try? How about many tries, or unlimited times? He would have the same chance the prophets had for those eight prophecies being fulfilled. Which is virtually no chance. That is calculating only eight of the prophecies of the over 200-plus prophecies! That is a very descriptive comparative story to explain how unreasonable it is to think the human conduits of God's holy Word in the Bible were not inspired by that same God.

Professor Stoner went on the become a staunch Christian apologist, concluding after the studies in his classroom. "Any man who rejects Christ as the Son of God is rejecting a fact proved perhaps more absolutely than any other fact in the world."[6]

---

[5] Peter W. Stoner, Science Speaks, Moody Press, Chicago, IL. 1957. Pgs 147-155

[6] Ibid, pg 112

What about all the rest of the prophecies and their odds? Calculated by the same students and explained in his same book, calculating 44 Messianic prophecies, the odds jump to 1 in 10^{147}. That's 147 zeros! All prophecies? Simply incalculable, except that the real Author of these prophecies knows the future. The God who created the universe out of nothing was in total control and knows the past, present *and* future.

Not all prophets, like self-anointed prophets today, speak the truth from God. *"Thus says the LORD of hosts, 'Do not listen to the words of the prophets who prophesy to you. They make you worthless; they speak a vision of their own heart, not from the mouth of the LORD.'"* **Jer 23:16** How is a true prophet identified? When every prophetic message comes true without failure, that is a true prophet. Failures? False prophets.

The writings by the major and minor prophets in the Bible which include the coming Christ are 100% accurate. There are also yet-to-be-filled prophecies, especially concerning His second coming. This record of accuracy is an overwhelming reason we *must* believe the Holy Bible is as it says it is. It gives us confidence that we can have faith the unfulfilled prophecies will come to fruition, just as Israel becoming a nation and Jesus' coming.

> *"No prophecy of Scripture is of any private interpretation, for prophecy **never came by the will of man, but holy men of God spoke as they were moved by the Holy Spirit**."* **2 Pet 1:20,21**

The Bible is authentic because it says it is! Arguments against that insist it is a circular argument. "The Bible is true because it says it is; it must be true because it is in the Bible." The above probability/odds needs no further verification that someone very Divine was and still is involved.

Rabbinical Judaism puts the life of Moses and his inspired writings from God around 1400B.C. Church of Ireland Archbishop James Ussher, in his detailed analysis of Biblical genealogies, puts Moses birth at 1592BC.[7] The first five books of the Old Testament are attributed to him, as well as the Book of Job. Moses lived 120-years, so his recordings were written anywhere from 1400-1592BC.

---

[7] James Ussher, *Annals of the World*, 1568.

God went silent through His prophets for 400 years[8] before the first coming of Jesus Christ. No computers to archive previous records, no prophets receiving new messages from God. New Testament writings commenced around 50A.D. and the final book Revelation attributed to the Apostle John was around 90-95A.D. Therefore, the Holy Bible was written over a period of about fifteen-sixteen hundred years, on three different continents, by at least forty different authors (most having no clue about the others or collusion within their writers groups), in at least three different languages. Get ready—all that with nary a contradiction!

That statement about "no contradictions" is often attacked by skeptics with all kinds of Scriptural evidence. Books and websites supporting both sides are prevalent. In reality, any discrepancy is minor and not one affects any part of the story of the Bible or the *Good News*. I was once one who challenged the authenticity of the Bible, researched all the "errors" to back up my and others' claims the Bible is bogus, and was subsequently slapped in the face by the Holy Spirit in my come-to-Jesus moment. Hallelujah! It is also noted that any discrepancy is easily understood and explained, but it is also important to acknowledge that the Word of God contains no errors. Any so-called errors can be attributed to man, even our own finite understanding.

The four gospels, Matthew, Mark, Luke, and John harmonize so well together. What one lacks in detail, the other fills in from a different perspective. These four books are the subject of some of those so-called contradictions or errors. Were there one, two angels at the tomb, three, or more? Simple answer to that is not one describes the scene as *only* two, or three, or more. And what does it matter, anyway!

My testimony of how the Holy Bible changed my life through my coming to Christ Jesus may not be enough to change someone else. Other infamous atheists and critics of the Bible had similar metamorphous changes, the likes of C.S. Lewis (atheist-to-apologist Christian author), Lee Strobel (a Chicago investigative reporter, *The Case For Christ* series), James W. Wallace (a cold case LAPD investigative detective, *Cold Case*

---

[8] The Deuterocanonical Books, also know as the Apocrypha, are writings through this 400-year period. Though not considered to have passed all Canonical standards, it is interesting reading, especially a fill-in-the-gap of Jewish history.

Christianity), multi-millionaire Michael McIntyre (all the money couldn't buy him peace and joy), Josh McDowell (*The New Evidence that Demands a Verdict*) and many, *many* others. Ironically, those just mentioned also tried to disprove the Bible once and for all, but came to the opposite conclusion, all becoming powerful apologists for the Word of God.

Admittedly, there are many who have left the faith and the Word of the Holy Bible. Ah-HAA! Another Biblical prophecy coming true!

> *"The Spirit expressly says that in latter times, some will depart from the faith, giving heed to deceiving spirits and doctrines of demons."* **1 Tim 4:1**

This world is filled with deceiving spirits and doctrines of demons with so many eager to jump in on that party train. Those who studied and practiced Christian faith for many years, only to bail, know the dangers and the warnings. No one can speak for those who defected, but they are responsible for the consequences of their eternal fate. Let me pause here for a moment: We must all pray for those people, the lost, those who do not know the path to their salvation, or have strayed from the Truth.

If the Holy Bible is not the inspired Word of God? Oh well, many believers like me will have lived their lives in peace and joy like no other and spreading it along the way. On the other hand, if the Bible is the Word of God? One cannot dodge the horrific Biblical consequences for eternity of denying the Father and our Lord Jesus Christ.

> *"For if, after they have escaped the pollutions of the world through the knowledge of the Lord and Savior Jesus Christ, they are again entangled in them and overcome, the latter end is worse for them than the beginning. For it would have been better for them not to have known the way of righteousness, than having known it, to turn from the holy commandment delivered to them. But it has happened to them according to the true proverb. 'A dog returns to his own vomit,' and, 'a sow, having washed, to her wallowing in the mire.'"* **2 Pet 2:20-24**

Better not to have known than having known.... I would not want to be one of the defectors, unrepentant backsliders, or those who turn their back to God. Let us pray.... The Bible is true, with its warnings, too!

Chapter 5: HEY, I WAS THERE!

While sitting at a traffic light several years ago, in the middle of the day, suddenly a man came running alongside the driver side of my vehicle, leaned across the hood, and began spraying shots at someone across the street. When these things happen, they happen so unexpectedly, shockingly, and one does not have time to comprehend what had just happened.

Eyewitness testimony in court is ultra-important in a prosecutor's case against a defendant. When called as a witness, I was expected to remember every detail as the defense attorney tries to blow holes in a witness's recollection of the episode.

The same is true when analyzing the authenticity of the Holy Bible and its character witnesses. Many Bible "prosecutors" have tried to discredit its contents, the stories, and vital characters. Unsuccessfully, I might add.

The main character in the Bible, from Genesis through Revelation, is Jesus our Christ, our Lord and Savior. Yes, His presence was throughout the Old Testament, also, many eyewitnesses in both the Old and New Testament.

The books attributed to Matthew, Mark, and John were authored by these eyewitnesses to Jesus, His miracles, His sharing the Gospel—the Good News, and His suffering and eventual crucifixion on the cross at Calvary. They wrote about their walk alongside the Messiah each in their individual way, yet convincingly without reproach that this Man is the Christ, the Savior of the world. These were real people in real historical time in real historical places and their testimonies have held up through incredible scrutiny throughout all these centuries.

How could this simple, humble Man be the Savior of the world? How could the Jews have "missed" Him? He certainly did not fit the description the Jews had envisioned as the coming Christ, the King of Kings, so they rejected Him.

According to Matthew, Mark, and John, the reigning kings feared He was the King to supplant their authority, acknowledging that He was the King of Kings. *"Then King Herod heard this, he was disturbed and all Jerusalem with him, he had called together all the people's chief priests and teachers of the law, he asked where the Messiah was to be born."* Matt 2:3,4 After the birth of Christ, King Herod *"gave orders to kill all boys in Bethlehem and its vicinity who were two years old and under, in accordance with the time he had learned from the Magi."* Matt 2:16 He realized this young child King was a threat to his own kingship.

These three Apostles and the others walked alongside Jesus during His ministry here on earth as the only begotten Son of our living God. Jesus asked them who the people thought He was, then He asked, *"But who do you think I am?"* Simon Peter answered, *"You are the Christ, Son of the living God."* Matt 16:15,16

More and more gathered to witness His miracles, His wisdom, His power and His love, and the warnings of not following Him. *"I am the Way, the Truth, and the Life; no one comes to the Father except through Me."* Jn 14:6

There are many who doubted and denied His deity, but in the end, the enemy centurion said, *"Truly this was the Son of God."* Matt 27:54

It is generally believed that Luke was a doctor near Antioch, likely a companion of Saul's (Paul) and his perspective of this Man, God manifested in the flesh, is different than the Apostles that walked amongst Jesus. While the others were of Jewish persuasion, Luke comes on the scene as a Gentile, a physician, familiar with details and brings another angle to the life of our Christ with intuitive insight.

The four Gospels, including that of Luke, align well with each other. It is unlikely that Luke was an associate companion of the other three, but it is believed that Luke used a portion of the Book of Mark as a reference.

> *"But Peter and the other apostles answered and said: "We ought to obey God rather than men. The God of our fathers raised up Jesus whom you murdered by hanging on a tree. Him God has exalted to His right hand to be Prince and Savior, to give repentance to Israel and forgiveness of sins. And we are His witnesses to these things, and so also is the Holy Spirit whom God has given to those who obey Him.*

HEY, I WAS THERE!

An often-overlooked passage regarding a testimony of Jesus Christ as an eternally-existing Son of God is one recognized by a religious enemy of Jesus.

> *"When they heard this,* [the council of Rome] *they were furious and plotted to kill them. Then one in the council stood up, a Pharisee named Gamaliel, a teacher of the law held in respect by all the people, and commanded them to put the apostles outside for a little while. And he said to them: 'Men of Israel, take heed to yourselves what you intend to do regarding these men. For some time ago Theudas rose up, claiming to be somebody. A number of men, about four hundred, joined him. He was slain, and all who obeyed him were scattered and came to nothing. After this man, Judas of Galilee rose up in the days of the census, and drew away many people after him. He also perished, and all who obeyed him were dispersed.*
>
> *And now I say to you, keep away from these men and let them alone; for if this plan or this work is of men, it will come to nothing; but if it is of God, you cannot overthrow it--lest you even be found to fight against God.'"* **Acts 5:29-39**

Two thousand years later, this Man whom His followers claimed to be Christ, remains the living Foundation of Christianity that has grown throughout the world. It did not cease when Jesus died. Why not? Because firsthand eyewitness testimonies of those who witnessed not just Jesus in the flesh, but everything He is as the Self-Existent One.

Every detail of the Jesus story exceeds any challenges of credibility of who He was, and is, and is to come. No one, not Steven King, Dean Koontz, John Grisham, nor any other fiction authors could ever have created a story line so compelling or as accurate from the beginning to the end of His life here on earth. Our King beyond a reasonable doubt.

Gamaliel was an intelligent, spiritual leader and I am certain he knew who Jesus was, the real deal, and His followers would go to the grave with Him. Many more would jump on the bandwagon, unlike the results of believing in the many imposters before and after His coming. Gamaliel was correct. His coming was of God, and man cannot stop it.

Chapter 6: WOULD YOU DIE FOR A LIE?

There are many incredible stories in the Holy Bible about testing one's faith. Even after all these 2000 years since the crucifixion, burial, and resurrection from the dead, Jesus maintains His power of residency inside all those who believe, through the Holy Ghost. Throughout the centuries, martyrs have willingly given up their own lives for He who is in us.

All of the original Apostles, except John, were martyred, unwilling to relinquish their faith. Tradition says that even John was dropped in boiling oil yet survived by the miracles of God Almighty. Why are people so eager to lay down their life for Christ? Because of the belief that He is the Messiah and there is no greater sacrifice. Eternal life with Him is the promise.

Many know the story from the Book of Daniel wherein three servant-slaves defiantly refused to bow to the gods of Nebuchadnezzar and his mighty statue.

> *"Shadrach, Meshach, and Abednego, answered and said to the king, 'O Nebuchadnezzar, we are not careful to answer thee in this matter. If it be so, our God whom we serve is able to deliver us from the burning fiery furnace, and he will deliver us out of thine hand, O king.* <u>*But if not, be it known unto thee, O king, that we will not serve thy gods, nor worship the golden image which thou hast set up.*</u>*'"* **Dan 3:16-18**

The underlined in that passage is important and often understated. They were willing to get thrown into the fiery furnace even knowing that the probability of their death by fire was likely imminent. *"But if not...."* That was the faith they had that either way, God would be with them.

> *"Then these men were bound in their coats, their hosen, and their hats, and their other garments, and were cast into the midst of the burning fiery furnace. ...Lo, I see four men loose, walking in the midst of the fire, and they have no hurt; and the form of the fourth is like the Son of God. Then Shadrach, Meshach, and Abednego, came forth of the midst of the fire. And the princes, governors, and captains, and the king's counsellors, being gathered together, saw these men, upon whose bodies the fire had no power, nor was a hair of their head singed, neither were*

> *their coats changed, nor the smell of fire had passed on them."*
> **Dan 3:21, 25-27**
>
> *Nebuchadnezzar spoke, saying, "Blessed be the God of Shadrach, Meshach, and Abed-Nego, who sent His Angel and delivered His servants who trusted in Him, and they have frustrated the king's word, and yielded their bodies, that they should not serve nor worship any god except their own God! Therefore I make a decree that any people, nation, or language which speaks anything amiss against the God of Shadrach, Meshach, and Abed-Nego shall be cut in pieces, and their houses shall be made an ash heap; because there is no other God who can deliver like this."* **Dan 3:28,29**

Fairy tale? Daniel wrote firsthand of this testimony with such detail. The accuracy of his prophetic writings throughout the Book of Daniel give credibility to the reality of this episode and his other experiences.

Stephanus, a disciple of Jesus, gave a long dissertation of the reason for his faith shortly before his last breath, being stoned to death. His last words, *"Lord, do not charge them with this sin."* **Acts 7:60**

The Apostle Paul, formerly known as Saul who stood over the stoning of Stephanus, went through an incredible conversion. He saw much privilege as one of the highest ranking officers in the Roman army, yet on his way to Jerusalem to crucify all those peaceful, believing Christians, he was knocked off his horse, blinded, and heard the voice of God, testifies to one-on-one counseling by Jesus Christ Himself, and authored at least 13 of the epistles in the New Testament.

He could have lived his life in comfort as a respected leader, but his visions were so clear he could only serve ONE—Jesus Christ. Paul spoke of the trials and tribulations he faced after his conversion:

> *"I am more: in labors more abundant, in stripes above measure, in prisons more frequently, in deaths often. From the Jews five times I received forty stripes minus one. Three times I was beaten with rods; once I was stoned; three times I was shipwrecked; a night and a day I have been in the deep; in journeys often, in perils of waters, in perils of robbers, in perils of my own countrymen, in perils of the Gentiles, in perils in the city, in perils in the wilderness, in perils in the sea, in perils*

among false brethren; in weariness and toil, in sleeplessness often, in hunger and thirst, in fastings often, in cold and nakedness—" **2 Cor 11:22-33**

Paul could have sat back and collected his social security and enjoyed a nice retirement, but he became the most zealous of them all for the Gospel of Jesus Christ, eventually, being be-headed. Paul had a first-hand encounter with Jesus that changed him radically for Christ. Though maybe not as dramatic, many of us have had direct encounters with Jesus.

My ministry name is "Forty Less One," a reference to the five times that Paul was whipped in horrific fashion (2 Cor 11:24), yet none of that deterred his mission of the Gospel in Christ Jesus. Could I remain as faithful? The name *Forty Less One* is always a reminder that challenges my conscience, if faced with martyrdom, would I be willing….

Throughout the centuries, there have been those who claimed to be the true second coming of the Messiah, several in our lifetime.

David Koresh was one such character who had an entire community of followers at then Davidian Branch in Waco, TX, (1993) Cult leader Jim Jones started his own camp he called Jonestown in Guyana (1978). Both camps ended tragically, with murders, suicides, and government assault (Waco). Jones and Koresh both died just like many imposters before and after, even today. None of them arose from the dead with witnesses and verification. Jesus did.

Just as Gamaliel had suggested nearly 2000 years ago, *it will come to nothing; but if it is of God, you cannot overthrow it--lest you even be found to fight against God."* **Acts 5:29-39** It *has* come to something.

Christianity has continued and survived as Gamaliel had expected; it did not come to nothing but the most popular religion in the world. While consensus does not make something true, the fact that many believe and deny themselves, take up their cross, and follow Him is compelling.

Throughout the centuries, people willing to die in defense of their belief and love in Jesus is in the millions. There are more martyrs today than any time in history. We are fortunate that in this great country the United States of America, we can practice religious freedom without threat of imprisonment or death, but that is not true in other parts of the world. Missionaries daily risk their very own precious lives to go into such areas to spread the Gospel of Jesus Christ. Would they die for a lie?

Chapter 7: A LOOK FROM THE OUTSIDE

The Holy Bible has been the most scrutinized publication yet sustains as the most credible compilation of writings ever assembled. So far in this book, the evidence has been primarily from within the Bible itself.

> *"Without controversy, great is the mystery of Godliness. God was manifested in the flesh, justified in the Spirit, seen by angels, preached among the Gentiles, believed on in the world, and received up in glory."* **1 Tim 3:16**

Paul was face-to-face with our Savior and wrote the above convincing passage after being ministered to by the Most High. There is no doubt that such testimonies are powerful in substantiating the authenticity of the Bible. But now, let's start looking outside the Bible.

Many people and witnesses outside the Holy Bible affirm that Jesus was a real person, yet something specifically peculiar about Him. Flavius Josephus was a well-respected historian of the day and had a front row seat to the destruction of Rome. He was born about 37A.D. into a priestly family of Jews. His early adult years were at war on the side of the Israel and the Jews as they fought against the Greco-Roman empire. When the Romans destroyed Israel and Josephus became a captive, he switched sides to the Roman guard. His defection did not diminish his attempts to record history as he witnessed it or learned of it from the living Apostles and church fathers. This is an excerpt from his book "Antiquities of the Jews."

> Now there was about this time Jesus, a wise man, [if it be lawful to call him a man]; for he was a doer of wonderful works, a teacher of such men as receive the truth with pleasure. He drew over to him both many of the Jews and many of the Gentiles. [He was the Christ]. And when Pilate, at the suggestion of the principal men amongst us, had condemned him to the cross, those that loved him at the first did not forsake him; for he appeared to them alive again the third day; as the divine prophets had foretold these and ten thousand other wonderful things

concerning him. And the tribe of Christians, so named from him, are not extinct at this day.[9]

Josephus also mentions other Biblical characters such as John the Baptizer, acknowledges James as the brother of Jesus, Pontius Pilate, Tiberias, Herod the Great, Herod Antipas, Caiaphas, and others, corroborating the authenticity of the Holy Bible.

Justin [Martyr] was another early apologist for the Christian faith. He lived at a time when Christianity was powerfully hanging on after the turn of the first century and many of the stories of Jesus' life were fresh in the people's minds. A philosopher in the early-mid second century, his own conversion was commenced. "A fire was suddenly kindled in my soul. I fell in love with the prophets and these men who had loved Christ; I reflected on all their words and found that this philosophy alone was true and profitable. That is how and why I became a philosopher. And I wish that everyone felt the same way that I do."[10]

Eventually, he and his Christian acquaintances were arrested and asked to denounce their faith but were beheaded when unwilling to do so. Thus, his surname became Martyr.

Anyone who tries to deny Jesus was a real person in the first century has his/her head in the sand because the evidence *outside* the Bible is overwhelming.

The extensive list below is only a sample of the many other historical sources outside of the Bible that corroborate details within the Bible, verifying its authenticity.

- Long life spans prior to the Flood[11]
- The confusion of language as we have in the Biblical account of the Tower of Babel (Gen 11:1–9)

---

[9] Flavius Josephus, *Antiquities of the Jews,* Antiquities 18, Chapter 3, Section 3. The bracketed sections were suspected of having been put in by Christian influences during translation from Greek to English. But if true, does not change Josephus's own recognition of Jesus as a peculiar person.

[10] Quote, unsourced, Attributed to him in most Christian circles.

[11] Many believe that the old ages people lived prior to the flood, i.e. Methuselah at 960 years old, were just myths. But Bible consistency between its authors and other comparable accuracies would imply otherwise.

- The Exodus as confirmed by the Roman historian Tacitus and Josephus (who also quotes an Egyptian historian named Manetho who mentions it)
- The campaign into Israel by Pharaoh Shishak (1 Kings 14:25–26), as recorded on the walls of the Temple of Amun in Thebes, Egypt
- Revolt of Moab against Israel (2 Kings 1:1, 3:4–27), as recorded on the Mesha Inscription (also known as the Moabite Stone) in the Louvre Museum
- Fall of Samaria (2 Kings 17:3–6, 24, 18:9–11) to Sargon II, king of Assyria, as recorded on his palace walls
- Defeat of Ashdod by Sargon II (Isaiah 20:1), as recorded on his palace walls
- Campaign of the Assyrian king Sennacherib against Judah (2 Kings 18:13–16), as recorded on the Taylor Prism in the British Museum
- Siege of Lachish by Sennacherib (2 Kings 18:14, 17), as recorded on the Lachish reliefs
- Assassination of Sennacherib by his own sons (2 Kings 19:37), as recorded in the annals of his son Esarhaddon
- Fall of Nineveh as predicted by the prophets Nahum (1:1–3:19) and Zephaniah (2:13–15), as recorded on the Tablet of Nabopolassar in the British Museum
- Fall of Jerusalem to Nebuchadnezzar, king of Babylon (2 Kings 24:10–14), as recorded in the Babylonian Chronicle Tablets
- Captivity of Jehoiachin, king of Judah, in Babylon (2 Kings 24:15–16), as recorded on the Babylonian Ration Records
- Fall of Babylon to the Medes and Persians (Daniel 5:30–31), as recorded on the Cyrus Cylinder in the British Museum
- Freeing of captives in Babylon by Cyrus the Great (Ezra 1:1–4; 6:3–4), as recorded on the Cyrus Cylinder
- The revolt against Rome led by "Judas of Galilee" the founder of the Zealots (Acts 5:37) as recorded by Josephus
- The prolonged mid-day darkness on the day Jesus died (Mark 15:33), as recorded by the Roman historian Thallus (c. AD 50),

- a Greek author named Phlegon, Julius Africanus, and Tertullian
- The "great famine" in Israel (**Acts 11:28**) as recorded by Josephus, Tacitus, and Suetonius
- The expulsion of the Jews from Rome by the emperor Claudius (**Acts 18:2**) as recorded by Suetonius

Every one of those events is verifiable from outside-the-Bible sourcing. It is often said by some Christians that the Bible is not a history book. Why not? On the contrary, many secular world history books have used the Holy Bible as their own sourcing, and the accuracy of the Bible is uncanny as the authenticity of events in the Bible have been substantiated beyond a reasonable doubt.

Dedicated archaeologists, with their tiny brushes and excavation tools, uncover artifacts and evidence of events recorded in history, the history lessons of the sacred book. More often, they prove all that is in the Bible to be factual.

No other book in history ever has self-proven its relevancy and authenticity more than the Holy Bible. Not the Quran, not gold tablets of Joseph Smith and his Book of Mormon (or his other SDA books); not Ellen G. White's books, only the Bible. But that should not surprise anyone because it is the *only* book truly inspired by the Holy Spirit and God's human messengers.

The Bible survives because of its inerrant accuracy and the power and effect His Word has in people's lives. None of us would be here if it were not for God's truths that give life, rest, peace and joy, inspire, give hope, and transcends love, His love for us, His love for even the lost, that they eventually might be called to come to Him. All of this accomplished across cultural and language boundaries, nationalities and races, and the poor and the wealthy.

In the last fifty years, there has been an infatuation with publishing new and improved Holy Bibles, a new version coming out about every two-five years. This diminishes the original Word and opens the door to more Bible scrutiny and accuracy of translations and interpretations.

Chapter 8: DIGGING UP THE EVIDENCE

Naysayers doubt the Bible's authenticity because they ignorantly suggest that "it is just a book written by men." On the contrary, it is a book that contains many details of history thousands of years ago, verified by accurate and fulfilled prophecies beyond mathematical odds and archaeological discovers that confirm much of the historical background.

One of the most important discoveries throughout the centuries was in 1946 when some Bedouin shepherds found some ancient Jewish scrolls dated at the end of the first century, in an area about 13 miles east of Jerusalem and about 1300 feet below sea level. For about ten years, these caverns were excavated and extensively searched until about 825-870 fragments of scrolls were verified, both Biblical and unbiblical.

The importance of this find is that many of the scrolls were intact enough to accurately parallel many of the original writings as accurate, including complete sections of the prophet Isaiah.

➢ There are now identified among the scrolls, 19 copies of the Book of Isaiah, 25 copies of Deuteronomy and 30 copies of the Psalms.

➢ Prophecies by Ezekiel, Jeremiah and Daniel *not* found in the Bible are written in the Scrolls.

➢ The Isaiah Scroll, found relatively intact, is 1000 years older than any previously known copy of Isaiah. The scrolls are the oldest group of Old Testament manuscripts ever found.

➢ In the Scrolls are found never before seen psalms attributed to King David and Joshua.

➢ There are paraphrases that expand on the Law, rule books of the community, war conduct, thanksgiving psalms, hymnic compositions, benedictions, liturgical texts, and sapiential (wisdom) writings.

➢ The Scrolls for the most part were written in Hebrew, but there are many in Aramaic, the common language of the Jews for the last two centuries B.C. and of the first two centuries A.D. The discovery of the Scrolls has greatly enhanced our knowledge of these two languages. In addition, there are a few texts written in Greek.

Skeptics will say that these discoveries prove nothing, only that the writings were authenticated but had nothing to do with proving the Holy Bible is real and the sacred Word of God.

True, to a point, but just substantiating the prophecies to be as written certainly solidifies the Bible as accurate beyond human capabilities.

Every year, new uncoverings are discovered to verify historical truths as described in the Bible, again, taking the Bible from that being written by man to inspired by a Supreme Being.

- ✓ Sepulcher of Jesus. There had been suspicions where Jesus was entombed, then walked away from it, arisen from the dead. Today, excavators believe they have found the place where the body of Jesus was placed.

- ✓ Pool of Siloam. One of the numerous miracles detailed in the Book of John describes how Jesus healed a man who was born blind. "[Jesus] spit on the ground, made some mud with the saliva, and put it on the man's eyes. 'Go,' He told him, 'wash in the Pool of Siloam.' So the man went and washed, and came home seeing." Jn 9:7

    Biblical skeptics and critics claimed that this episode, and many other accounts of Christ's miracles, was pure fiction. The discovery of the Pool of Siloam, however, made that belief hard to uphold. Engineers stumbled upon the steps of a first century ritual pool in 2004 when they were working near the mouth of Hezekiah's Tunnel. Investigators found coins in the plaster of the pool dated back to the time of Jesus' life and death. By 2005, archaeologists said that this was undoubtedly the Pool of Siloam.

- ✓ Typically, the older something is, the more difficult it is to prove. The challenges of proving the Old Testament true has not stopped archaeologists from searching for answers to ancient questions. It has also not stopped them from finding said evidences and answers to historical questions.

    Ezra and 2 Chronicles both report that Cyrus the Great of Persia allowed the exiled Jews in Babylon to return to Israel after he conquered Babylonia. This unusually tolerant policy has raised questions for decades about whether Cyrus the Great allowed this to happen or if this was a fictitious episode. A nine-inch clay cylinder from 539 B.C., however, details not only Cyrus' victory over Babylon but his unexpected decision to allow Babylonia captives to return to their own ancestral homelands and rebuild their temples.

✓ Ancient coins found featuring King David and Julius Caesar, as well as other kings, prove that these were real people that did exist, and validate their existence in Biblical timelines.

✓ As inscriptions go, a 1993 discovery at Tel Dan established additional harmony with the Bible. A ninth century B.C. stone stela unearthed at Tel Dan carried the first evidence found outside the Bible for the existence of King David. The inscription was carved by an Aramean king who claimed to have defeated his two southern neighbors, the "king of Israel" and the "king of the House of David."

✓ In 2015, archaeologists in Israel discovered a bulla, the clay impression of a seal, that belonged to King Hezekiah. Ten feet away was another bulla. This one bore the name "Isaiah." The Isaiah of the Bible was Hezekiah's advisor in the late 8th and early 7th centuries B.C. As such, it would be no surprise to find the fate of these two men remained intertwined even in death. In an even more exciting twist, the name "Isaiah" was followed by the Hebrew letters "NVY." A prevailing theory is that "NVY" would have been followed by the Hebrew letter aleph. If this were true, the seal would spell out what would translate to "Isaiah the Prophet."

The list of archaeology finds continue to solidify, not weaken, the authentication of the Holy Bible. Every year, new discoveries continue to support stories inside the inspired writings in this most sacred book we know as the Holy Bible.

Many of the archaeologists are not Christians seeking to prove Biblical truths, so they are unbiased in their research. Many use the Holy Bible as a map to find the hidden treasures of ancient history. No doubt many do their work with an appreciation of the Bible's accuracy and countless have come to accept the Bible as Truth because of their work.

Chapter 9: BUT WHAT ABOUT ALL THE OTHER RELIGIONS?

The Holy Bible has survived so much interrogation and scrutiny and that in itself should prove the Bible's authenticity for almost 2,000 years, it continues to be the most important literary work in the entire world, across language and cultural barriers.

Christianity is not the only religion, so how and why have the others been able to flourish, or even survive, for hundreds, thousands of years. Judaism is the forerunner of Christianity as Christianity has its roots in the TORAH and the TANAKH or, the Hebrew Bible (Old Testament.)

The Quran is the Islam holy book, written by an illitcrate "prophet" named Mohammad in the middle seventh century. Mohammad self-claims to have been the "last prophet," and is one of the fastest growing religions of the world. But Mohammad never spoke any prophecy that was fulfilled, except his self-fulfilled pilgrimage to Mecca. So why is there so much allegiance to Allah, the Islam god?

While the Holy Bible survives continuous nuclear attacks from all angles, the Quran faces no such scrutiny, a real conundrum, in my opinion. Basic Biblical comparisons to the Quran:

THE HOLY BIBLE	THE QURAN
1) Written by at least 40 authors, over about 1700 years	1) Written by only one person, by Mohammad's wife as he dictated his visions to her
2) About 2500 prophecies, 2000 FULFIILED prophecies, includes over 200 Messianic	2) No fulfilled prophecies
3) Jesus was crucified, died, buried, arose from the dead	3) Mohammad's physical remains are still in the ground
4) The Bible is unchanging without errors or contradictions	4) The Quran has undergone several transitions, even by Mohammad himself

Given the nature of Arabic during Muhammad's life, much of the Quran was not written but orally known, and by memory. Muhammad would recite the same verse multiple ways, and so would his followers. He would also cancel previous texts through so-called *abrogation*: Muhammad would tell his followers that certain portions of the Quran he had relayed before were no longer to be recited as part of the Quran.

Therefore, if Muhammad needed part of the text to go away, he would replace it with another and tell his followers to stop reciting the earlier text and forget it. The Bible never underwent this sort of abrogation.

This may surprise you but today's Quran, which was not put together by one of the teachers Muhammad named, is but one of multiple Quranic canons, the ones that received official approval by the caliphate and became the standard text when the rest were burned. The first burning of the Quran was actually ordered by the third Caliph Uthman, who recalled all the variant manuscripts, about six of them, destroyed them by fire, and issued an official, standardized version according to *his* reading.[12]

There are many troubling practices that Muslims believe and often deny are in their sacred book. If the Quran would go through as much vetting as the Holy Bible, I suspect that it could not survive as a viable, believable religion.

Joseph Smith, accredited with founding of Mormonism, (also commonly called Church of Latter-Day Saints, or LDS) claimed to have been led by the angel Moroni in 1823 to a set of golden plates buried near his home. According to his own testimony, he took the plates home and translated them in his "Book of Mormon," published in 1830.

Smith made sure he had "eyewitness" testimonies available, so he gathered eleven associates to "view" and "verify" the plates. Their testimonies varied on seeing the plates, most admitted only to seeing a "pile" of "something" hidden under a blanket that Smith said was done so to protect the plates. When Smith was challenged in court, the testimony of these eleven so-called eyewitnesses was very inconsistent and had serious contradictions to each other's stories.

Mormons do not have a single reference book, but aside from the Holy Bible (which becomes backstage in their teachings), LDS has the Book of Mormon, Book of Doctrine and Covenants, and The Pearl of Great Price, all written by Joseph Smith. Like the Quran, the foundation of this religion is one man who also claimed to be the last prophet, with no fulfilled prophecies, except an approaching Civil War between the

---

[12] Many websites verify this had happened and its purpose was a "cleansing" of the different versions, a unification, of sorts.

North and South. That could easily have been speculated and predicted, considering the tensions that were mounting within the young country.

Mormons are wonderful people, very generous with their time and assets, yet those credentials do not prove validity to their core sources of reference that supersede the Bible. The golden plates have never been found, and unlike proof of ancient manuscripts of the Bible, the plates come with them much speculation and suspicion.

Joseph Smith did end up in the court room many times for fraud, and his own claim that he could read and translate Hebrew was declared fraudulent and deceptive to his followers. Most LDS members do not know his history because it's mostly been scrubbed from their teachings.

Step right up, Jehovah's Witnesses; your turn to be grilled! Charles Taze Russel is the founder of the Jehovah's Witnesses. The JWs are a spin-off from the early Adventist movement in the 19th Century when Baptist preacher William Miller predicted the coming of Christ and the end of the world in 1843. The group separated into many splinter groups, Charles Taze Russell starting the Jehovah's Witnesses in 1879. His prophecy that the world would end in 1914 obviously was wrong, also.

Many failed false prophecies, especially their several predictions of the earth's ending dates and Jesus' coming have forced them to amend that their prophecies were not failures, but *misinterpretations*. The Watchtower Society is the sovereign word of what JWs should believe.

Seventh Day Adventists? Ellen G. White, a prophetess who had similar visions like Joseph Smith (less the gold plates), proposed similar doctrines and failed prophecies. Their own "visons" are believed supreme over the Bible, yet JW's, LDSs, SDAs all claim the Bible is the inerrant Word of God while putting their doctrines above the Bible.

Now enter all the different Christian denominations, *different*, the key. Four simple words of two distinct scenarios: God said; man said.

Jesus Christ established *His* Church. Does Jesus ever fail? No, His Church will not fail. His Church is consistent, without controversy. I have heard it spoken by well-meaning Christians: "There is no perfect church." *His* Church is perfect. The problem is that we have turned His perfect Church into a hodge-podge of so much confusion, so far adrift from His perfect Church. Humans did that, not Christ, ignoring the consistent guidance from the Holy Bible and Holy Ghost.

That confusion is also what drives many wedges between Christians. The emphasis should be on getting back to what the Bible *actually* says, not what we selfishly want it to read. God said, man said.

Many Christian groups and denominations create divisions amongst themselves and give ammunition to those who want to tear the Bible to shreds with claims that the Bible is not the inspired Word of God. God does care about what people think about His holy Word; He demands that we accept it as His means of communicating to us and through us.

Hinduism is regarded to be the oldest religion of the world, guesstimated to have begun between 2300BC to 1500 B.C. Ironically, those dates include the window of when Abraham, Isaac, and Jacob and other early Bible characters would have been on the scene. Noah's flood was about 2345 B.C., so God was certainly working back then in His people.

The second oldest religion is considered to be Judaism, which we are familiar with as the Old Testament of the Bible. The early Hebrews-turned-Jews all respect and believe the "Law and the Prophets," the TORAH and the rest of the Old Testament as a whole. Tradition has the Jewish religion beginning about the seventh-eighth centuries B.C., and of course, Christianity followed from Judaism into the New Testament teachings of Jesus Christ our Lord and Savior. Jews: turn one more page.

Why this brief lesson about various religions, the source of their beliefs, and denominations? While the Bible is still scrutinized and challenged even today, all these other writings/gold plates have not faced the same challenges, especially the Quran. Yet, they fail in comparison to the evidence contained in the Holy Bible for their own claims to be from God, like the Holy Bible, the sovereign inspired Word of God.

Incidentally, in trying to research the oldest manuscripts in world history? The memoirs of Moses, whether oral or written, in the Old Testament, transferred to future generations, appear to be the oldest *surviving* manuscripts, whether religious or secular. It is no wonder as God had His hands in preserving every Word for all future testimonies and witnesses. Amen.

> The Holy Bible can restore one's life, give peace, hope and joy like no other book, and is a roadmap to eternal life in a glorified body, with Jesus.

CLOSING:

The Holy Bible is obviously true and accurate in every aspect, including His promises and prophetic messages. Its relevancy in today's confused world becomes even more significant as we get closer to His promised return.

Educated people assume that science and modern philosophies have replaced the Bible. Wrong on so many fronts. Sadly, many dismiss the Bible's content as fables and fantasies, yet every detail of the Bible has been verified somehow, someway, somewhere, through God's prophets, His witnesses, and promises and physical evidence.

To believe in the Bible is not blind faith, but faith in the substance of things hoped for, the evidence of things not seen. It is not, "God said it, so it is…," but more, *"Thus saith the LORD…"* and *proved* it all. That kind of faith is powerful and is reinforced by recorded real-time first-hand witnesses, historical recollections, physical evidence in the archaeological discoveries, how the Bible has changed individuals, and all the power that is extended through believers in our Lord and Savior Jesus Christ.

Paul said, *"Examine yourselves whether you are of the faith. Test yourselves. Do you not know that Christ Jesus is in you? Unless indeed, you are disqualified."* 2 Cor 13:5 Christ is in you, and what glorious love from our Creator that is!

I hope this book has been a blessing to you and included basic information that you can use to defend your faith in the Bible's authenticity. Whether people accept your defense of the Holy Bible is not on you, but on them, their free will choice. You know the influence and power the Bible has had in your own life, family members, and friends. You may, hopefully and prayerfully, just turn a few people to come to Jesus to receive all His promises, including eternal life with our Savior. What a glorious day that will be!

Is the Holy Bible true? The final answer is… THE BIBLE IS TRUE! And, beyond a reasonable doubt.

Share the Good News!

May the God of all grace, mercy, peace, and love bless you abundantly.

What is the most valuable point of discussion in this book that you can use to defend the Holy Bible as the authentic Word of God to others?

IS THIS YOUR "COME TO JESUS" MOMENT?

If you are not a born again Christian, make this a part of your story. The so-called sinners' prayer is an opening to your new journey as a Christian--welcome to the family. Remember that this is just the beginning of you becoming and continuing a lifelong Christian commitment, with new life and assurance of eternal life in beautiful heaven above with Jesus in all His glory. Already born again? Use this prayer during your witnessing and bringing others to saving-faith.

"Father, I know that I have broken your laws and my sins have separated me from you. I am truly sorry and now I want to turn away from my past sinful life toward You in repentance. Please forgive me and help me avoid sinning again. I believe that your only begotten Son Jesus the Christ, died for my sins, was resurrected from the dead, is alive, and hears my prayer.

I invite Jesus, to become the Lord of my life, to rule and reign in my heart from this day forward. Please send your Holy Spirit to help me know and believe who You are, obey You and all that you have commanded in Your holy Word, to put my trust in You only, to always put You above all things, to walk in this marvelous gift of the Holy Spirit within me and dissolve my desires to walk in the flesh, and to do Your will for the rest of my life.

This is not an emotional or temporary proclamation on my part, but a lifelong commitment to serve You and to live as Christ did, as I deny myself, take up my own cross, and follow You, Jesus, my Savior. Jesus, help me in directing my paths in your righteousness.

In Jesus' Almighty name I pray, Amen."

A true confession of faith is Biblically necessary. In the original Greek language, faith and belief are the same, and *continuous*. One, therefore, must believe that the Bible is true, and walk in that faith.

Now it's up to you to walk the walk, talk the talk, and live a life that exemplifies your new creation in Christ Jesus. May our living God bless you and your family abundantly. Amen.

Other books by author John J. Briggle

The Omega Times A fiction novel (or is it?) about a Christian family who suffers family tragedy, then endures in a carnal world, eventually witnessing first-hand the end times cometh. Suspenseful with parallel stories going on at the same time, with twists and turns.

Why Am I Here? Without a doubt, you have asked yourself this question at least one time. The book begins with the author's own testimony, followed by topics such as evil in the world, why bad things happen to good people, and ultimately your own personal identity with your Creator.

Are You A True Christian? A provocative challenge to yourself to "examine yourself" and define your walk in Christ Jesus. Are you truly "doing" what the Holy Bible says? Ultimately, you and you alone are responsible for your salvation.

To Hell In A Handbasket A very critical book to read if you are concerned about your eternal destination, heaven or hell. This book debunks the "once saved-always saved" Calvinist myth. This is a must read to prevent you from being misled by those at the pulpit, TV ministries, Christian music, books, etc. The Holy Bible is the only source of absolute truth and I for one don't desire you to go "To Hell In A Handbasket."

Other books by author John J. Briggle

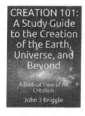

Creation 101: A Study Guide to the Creation of the Earth, Universe, and Beyond From a Biblical perspective, this book defends the basic reading of the Holy Bible and proposes to conform the sciences to the Bible rather than compromising with a worldview.

The Hidden Sacred Name Of God Do you know God's real name? The Bible clearly says you should: "And God spoke to Moses and said, I am YAHVAH. I appeared to Abraham, Isaac, and to Jacob, as Almighty, but by My name YAHVAH I was not known." A basic study of His true name and why He should be praised as such.

Is King Solomon In Heaven? An exegesis challenge to whether or not the famous king lived up to God's plan for redemption and inheritance into His kingdom of heaven. Is it an important question to even ask?

Life Of A Golden Everyone loves their pets, right? From that goldfish to your four-legged dog or cat. A fun "autobiography" of Bella our golden retriever through her first 2 ½ years. An excellent childrens book to be shared with your loved ones of all ages.

Other books by author John J. Briggle

Books are available on Amazon.com and Kindle Books. Special pricing also now available.

Coming soon: Original Christian music by singer-songwriter and composer John J Briggle. *iTunes*, Spotify, Youtube, and your other favorite download area.

Check out John J. Briggle's original secular songs now available, too, featuring *"Daddy's Little Girl."** iTunes, Spotify, Youtube, Walmart, Target, or your favorite music store. Search **Daddy's Little Girl Briggle**. Thanks!

*(*Daddy's Little Girl,* a song that is a candidate to be played at every wedding, father-daughter dance, and for inspirational listening.)

Thank you in advance and may the God of all grace, mercy, peace and love bless you and your family abundantly.

Love you all!

John J. Briggle and Ginny A Briggle

Made in the USA
Middletown, DE
08 May 2023